essential careers™

Careers in Human Resources

Jeri Freedman

Rosen Publishing
New York

Published in 2014 by The Rosen Publishing Group, Inc.
29 East 21st Street, New York, NY 10010

First Edition

Library of Congress Cataloging-in-Publication Data

Freedman, Jeri.
Careers in human resources/Jeri Freedman.—First edition.
pages cm.—(Essential careers)
Includes bibliographical references and index.
Audience: Grade 7 to 12.
ISBN 978-1-4777-1791-2 (library binding)
1. Personnel management—Vocational guidance—Juvenile literature.
I. Title.
HF5549.F692 2014
658.30023—dc23

2013012402

Manufactured in Malaysia

CPSIA Compliance Information: Batch #W14YA: For further information, contact Rosen Publishing, New York, New York, at 1-800-237-9932.

contents

INTRO

Employees are the most important resource of today's organizations, and human resources is the business area responsible for the overall management of an organization's employees.

DUCTION

Beginning in the second half of 2008, the world entered a global economic downturn. In the years since, the economy has stabilized, but growth in companies' sales has been slow. As a result, companies have not needed to hire large numbers of people. Thus, substantial numbers of people are unemployed. Jobs can be difficult to find, and there is a great deal of competition for the job openings that are available. Looking for jobs at a time when the economy is stagnant can be challenging and stressful. Finding a job that is likely to remain secure even in tough economic times can go a long way toward making one feel secure.

Human resources is a field that offers a number of benefits to those seeking recession-proof jobs. Virtually every company and organization needs human resources personnel to hire, train, and assist employees. Consequently, it is a field with a great number of employment opportunities. Moreover, if one does have to find a new job, there are many openings for experienced human resources personnel. Human resources is a field that offers job opportunities for those with various levels of skill and education. Often it is possible to get an entry-level job directly out of high school or after taking a short training program. One can continue one's education while working. This field also offers a career path with increasing levels of responsibility. Therefore, as one gains experience or undertakes additional education, it is possible to advance.

Human resources professionals are responsible for many areas of employee functioning in modern organizations.

Today, human resources is far more than screening and hiring people. Human resources personnel help managers obtain the best employees and assist them in resolving issues. They assist employees in resolving problems and help them make the most of their careers. Human resources professionals help employees find resources, such as agencies that provide help, when they are having personal problems and ensure that they are treated fairly and safely within the company.

Except in rare cases of a corporate crisis or disaster, jobs in this field often have regular hours. Pay varies with the type and size of company or organization one works for, but is on par with other jobs in business, providing a steady income that is likely to increase over time. Many businesses and organizations also provide good benefits such as health insurance and tuition reimbursement to allow employees to continue their education. Finally, because of the universal need for human resources personnel, it is possible to find a job in an industry that is interesting and at a company of suitable size.

chapter 1

What Is Human Resources?

The history of the human resources field is provided here to give insight into why and how the field developed. Following this, the various types of functions performed by human resources professionals are described.

The History of Human Resources

Human resources (HR) has played an important role in the welfare of workers since the early part of the industrial era. Prior to the nineteenth century, most of the economy of Europe and North America consisted of farming and craftspeople. In the nineteenth century, the development of machines made it possible to produce goods in large quantities in factories. This period, called the Industrial Revolution, saw a vast movement of people from the countryside to cities to work in factories. At first, conditions in factories were completely unregulated. Men, women, and even children worked extremely long hours under very harsh and often unsafe conditions, and pay was very low. In response to these cruel conditions came the first form of human resources, called industrial welfare. People concerned about the poor working conditions campaigned for laws to protect workers. The first such laws were passed in the United

Kingdom, beginning with the Factory Act of 1802, which regulated working conditions for children. Some of the conditions it addressed included limiting the work hours of children under the age of fourteen to eight hours per day and to twelve hours per day for those from fourteen to eighteen years old. In addition, the law forbade companies from making the children sleep more than two to a bed and required children to be taught reading, writing, and arithmetic for four years. Many more such industrial welfare laws were passed throughout the nineteenth century.

In 1913, the Welfare Workers Association was formed. It was the predecessor to modern personnel and professional development organizations. During World War I (1914–1918), the government developed an interest in using military personnel in the most effective way possible. The government implemented the use of IQ tests and aptitude testing to

In this nineteenth-century canning factory in Biloxi, Mississippi, women and children arrived to work before dawn and worked long hours packing fish by hand.

identify where people would perform best. This process was the beginning of modern aptitude testing.

During World War II (1939–1945), interest increased in improving the recruitment, selection, training, and motivation of both military personnel and those working in factories that produced goods to support the war effort. In response to this need, personnel departments were established with staff specifically trained in these areas. There was also increased focus on employee health and safety and on policies on wages.

In the 1970s, personnel professionals became involved in labor negotiations with unions and legal issues governing employees. In the 1990s, personnel departments became human resources departments. The change in name marked a switch from being primarily concerned with recruiting and hiring employees to focusing on employee development. In the 1990s and 2000s, there was an increased emphasis on ensuring equal opportunity, protecting employees from harassment, and promoting cultural diversity in the workplace. These concerns further expanded the role of human resources personnel. Today's human resources function involves a range of activities that go well beyond hiring and firing people to helping people maximize their potential and helping keep businesses running smoothly.

In fact, today the role of human resources has become so complex that a number of firms now exist that specialize in handling various aspects of human resources for other companies. Some of these companies focus on the hiring of employees, locating and screening employees for companies. Others focus on the legal aspects of labor relations. Still others manage employee benefit programs. Thus, in addition to jobs with individual companies and organizations, one could find employment with a contract services company in the human resources field.

STAFFING A COMPANY

Human resources plays an important role in the locating, screening, and hiring of employees. The exact activities that are performed by the human resources staff vary from company to company, but the following are common. The human resources personnel meet with company and departmental managers to identify labor needs. Often they help managers create job descriptions for positions that need to be filled. They also create ads for job openings and place those ads in newspapers and online, and post or distribute information on job openings internally so that interested employees can apply as well.

HR professionals often conduct telephone interviews with prospective employees to identify those who have the right qualifications before arranging in-person interviews.

In some companies, incoming résumés from applicants go directly to department managers. In others, human resources staff members screen résumés. They go through the incoming résumés and choose those that most closely match the job requirements and then forward those to the manager. Once the manager chooses the applicants he or she would like to interview, human resources staff may contact the applicants to arrange the interviews. After the manager chooses a candidate, human resources may be responsible for creating a letter of agreement or contract for the job.

After a person is hired for a job, he or she will meet with a human resources employee to fill out forms for payroll taxes and benefits. The HR representative will also have the new hire sign any necessary legal documents, such as a noncompete agreement, which prevents an employee from competing with the company for a certain period after leaving the company, or a confidentiality agreement, which requires that the employee keep company information secret. The human resources staff member will also explain company policies and may provide new employees with a policy handbook.

Most companies perform at least annual performance reviews to establish how effectively employees are doing their jobs and to identify any areas that need improvement. Often human resources personnel develop and distribute a standard form for this process. They may also keep track of when evaluations are expected to be performed and inform managers when they are due. If the manager and employee disagree about aspects of an employee's performance, a member of human resources may work with them to resolve the issue. The department of human resources often develops policies for dealing with employee problems. For example, it may require documentation of serious employee problems that may lead to termination. If a manager has an issue with an employee that he or she feels is serious, such as chronic lateness, human resources may require written documentation of the problem and keep track of such documentation.

Orienting and Training Employees

Human resources personnel are responsible for various training activities. They are responsible for providing initial orientation to new employees. This initiation includes activities such as introducing employees to various facilities and personnel and providing them with initial information about the company and its procedures. Some types of companies require new employees to review safety or other material related to their specific industry or to view orientation videos. HR is responsible for creating or acquiring this material. In addition, HR may arrange training for specific groups of employees, bringing in speakers or holding training sessions or workshops. HR also works with individual employees to help them access additional training that will help them advance in their job. This is known as professional development.

In some industries, the federal government or state regulatory agencies require some types of employees to undergo testing to ensure that they can perform their jobs correctly and safely. For instance, those working with dangerous chemicals

An HR staff member supervises new employees' orientation, including ensuring they understand company policies and procedures, and obtaining required personal information.

may be required to undergo testing to ensure that they know how to handle them safely. It is the HR department's responsibility to see that relevant employees are trained and tested.

The Outlook for the Human Resources Field

According to the U.S. Bureau of Labor Statistics (BLS), the demand for human resource specialists is expected to grow 21 percent from 2010 to 2020, and the need for human resources managers is expected to grow 13 percent. The demand for training and development managers is expected to grow 15 percent over this period, and the demand for benefits managers is expected to grow slightly. If the economy begins to recover over the next decade, it is likely that many new businesses will be formed. This growth in business would create an increased demand for human resources personnel.

Policies and Procedures

Every company requires rules that control how employees and managers should behave in the workplace. Some rules relate to benefits. For example, there are rules for how vacation time is accrued and how employees request time off. Other rules cover proper behavior in the workplace. For instance, there are rules against sexually harassing other employees and a procedure for reporting violations. The collection of rules is called policies and procedures. Some policies are decided on by management, such as the use of sick days and availability of disability insurance, which is not legally required in most states. Others are the result of laws, such as equal opportunity laws, which guarantee fair treatment to women and minorities.

In most companies it is human resources' responsibility to produce a written collection of policies and procedures. In many companies the human resources department produces a booklet that is given to all employees that summarizes all the policies and procedures. When employees have a question about a policy or procedure, human resources will answer their questions. Violations of policy may occur from time to time, such as an employee experiencing harassment at work. When this happens, human resources will be called on to investigate the incident. The human resources staff must take appropriate action to correct the problem or discipline the person who violated the policy.

When an incident occurs in the workplace, a human resources staff member must investigate and document what occurred, who was involved, and what action was taken in response.

Benefits and Compensation

Human resources works with members of senior management to develop policies for compensation. Compensation includes pay in cash and in other items of value, such as company stock. Human resources works with managers to decide on the initial pay offered to employees and the process by which employees receive raises. Human resources also oversees the benefits a company offers. HR staff members negotiate with outside providers such as health insurance companies and financial services companies that manage 401(k) retirement plans. The staff reviews these companies' offerings to select the plans offered to employees. The human resources staff is then responsible for educating employees about the features and costs of the plans. If outside agencies are used for compensation or benefit services, the human resources staff oversees the activities of these companies.

EMPLOYEE RELATIONS

Both workplace and personal problems can affect employees' performance. HR is responsible for ensuring that employees of all genders and races can work in a safe environment and be free from harassment or intimidation. They must also ensure that the company complies with laws such as the equal employment opportunity laws, including Title VII of the Civil Rights Act of 1964, which forbids discrimination on the basis of race or gender, and the Americans with Disabilities Act, which requires companies to make reasonable accommodations so that people with disabilities can work. Human resources personnel must develop procedures ensuring that employees and managers comply with the tenets of these laws. If an employee files a complaint about a violation of an employment law or regulation, the human resources staff must investigate and take appropriate action.

Human resources staff is sometimes called on to assist employees with personal problems. Such problems could include domestic violence or drug or alcohol abuse. If such issues are affecting an employee, HR can help that person find assistance, such as a rehabilitation program for substance abuse or a social services agency that helps battered women. Why would companies want to do this? Assisting an employee helps

Among the responsibilities of HR staff members is ensuring compliance with regulations covering employees with disabilities, including seeing that reasonable adjustments to equipment are made to allow them to work.

the company as well as the person. Personal problems can affect an employee's performance of his or her job, which in turn affects the company's productivity. Failing to keep experienced employees is expensive in terms of lost expertise, as well as the financial costs of finding and training a replacement. Therefore, both the company and employee benefit when an employee can be helped rather than fired.

chapter 2

The Kinds of Jobs That Exist in HR

There are different types of human resources jobs. These jobs are found at large, medium-sized, and small companies; nonprofit organizations; and government agencies.

Human Resources Assistant/ Coordinator

HR assistants perform basic human resources functions related to recruiting and assisting employees. They may write and post online ads and arrange for placement of print ads. They provide employees with materials on benefits and policies. They also perform clerical functions to support HR activities. This is a good entry-level job for people- and detailed-oriented students who are not college-bound. Many human resources assistant jobs do not have specific educational requirements beyond a high school diploma. However, knowledge of Microsoft Word, Excel, and PowerPoint software is valuable, as are excellent typing and keyboarding skills. Therefore, it is helpful to take either a vocational clerical program in high school, or a secretarial program at a secretarial school or junior college. Many companies today have employees from different cultural backgrounds, so speaking a second language, especially Spanish, can be beneficial in landing a job. A related job with a slightly higher level of responsibility is human resources

Today's companies employ workers from many different countries and cultural backgrounds. The ability to communicate with employees in their native language is an advantage for HR professionals.

coordinator. This job generally requires either a two-year associate's degree or two or more years of previous human resources experience.

HUMAN RESOURCES ADMINISTRATOR

Human resources administrators perform the day-to-day functions of the HR department. They recruit, screen, interview, and place workers. They counsel employees and deal with discipline issues. They oversee the orientation and training of employees. They prepare and distribute company documents. They maintain employee records. In addition, they may plan and oversee company events. This position generally requires a four-year bachelor's degree in human resources or business.

HUMAN RESOURCES SPECIALISTS

Larger companies often employ specialists in particular areas, which becomes their full-time job. In addition, standalone firms in the human resources field employ people in these areas to perform particular functions for client companies. Such positions include:

- Benefits manager: This person develops a combination of benefits offered to employees, such as health insurance, disability insurance, tuition reimbursement, and 401(k) retirement plans. The benefits manager reviews offerings from various vendors, selects options, and monitors usage by employees. This position requires at least a bachelor's degree in business or finance.
- Pension fund manager: This person is responsible for overseeing the investments for the company's pension

fund, the money owed to retired employees. He or she works with brokers to invest money in various assets such as stocks and bonds, monitors the plan's performance, and makes changes as necessary. Pension fund managers must ensure compliance with government regulations. They also oversee the distribution of money from the pension fund to the company's retirees. This position requires at least a bachelor's degree in accounting or finance, and in many cases a master's degree is preferred.

• Search specialist/recruiter: Those in this position must locate and screen potential employees. They work with managers to establish the requirements for employees. They place online and print ads and network with other professionals to locate candidates for higher-level positions. They may carry out phone interviews with candidates prior to arranging on-site interviews. They may also assist with

Search specialists must locate potential employees. Today, much of this work is done online, posting job ads and reviewing résumés via computer.

the preparation of employment agreements and other hiring-related documentation. This position requires a bachelor's degree in human resources or business, or several years of relevant HR experience.

Human Resources Manager or Director

Human resources managers plan, direct, and coordinate the administrative functions of an organization. They oversee the lower-level human resources staff and set the procedures for performing HR activities. They consult with top executives on strategic planning. They serve as a link between an organization's management and its employees, receiving information from senior management and communicating it to the employees.

Rewards and Challenges of Human Resources

There are a number of benefits to working in human resources. In good times and bad, a company needs human resources staff, so the job has great security. In addition, it has a solid career path from entry-level to senior management, which is largely experienced-based. Therefore, one can advance to increasing levels of responsibility with higher pay as one gains experience. Except at the highest levels, it also offers regular hours, so it is a job one can do and still have time to spend with one's family. It can also provide the satisfaction of helping employees develop and advance and helping them work out professional or personal problems. If one does need to find another job in the field, the vast number of positions makes it easier to find a job in human resources than in many other fields. The major drawback is stress from dealing with employees who are having issues at work or who have to be fired or laid off.

HR managers are also responsible for general managerial functions. For example, they must prepare and track a departmental budget and approve purchases for the department. The human resources manager may also work with the company's in-house or independent legal counsel to establish company policies and resolve legal issues as well as companies hired to run payroll and manage company benefits. This position usually requires a bachelor's degree in human resources or business and several years of previous experience in human resources.

Those who head HR departments must brief senior management of their company on the current status of employees and future needs for planning and budgeting purposes.

VICE PRESIDENT OF HUMAN RESOURCES

Once one has gained extensive experience as a human resources director, one can advance to the level of vice president of human resources. This rank is a senior management position and is most often found in larger companies. Vice presidents of human resources are responsible for developing high-level policies for human resources, such as those covering pay, raises, and benefits. They may be involved in developing systems for

The vice president of human resources informs HR staff about changes in company policies and procedures that result from a merger with another company.

managing employee information. They must have a detailed understanding of the laws that relate to human resources and must make sure they are complied with. They may be responsible for developing company-wide strategies to motivate employees and improve productivity. In the case of major organizational changes, such as a merger with another company, the vice president of human resources will be involved in designing the plan for organizing the combined employees. Those in this position must have at least a bachelor's degree in human resources or business, and some companies require a master's degree in business administration. This position also frequently requires many years of previous HR experience.

chapter 3

Headhunting and Other Jobs at HR Companies

Nearly all enterprises, except the very smallest, carry out some HR functions themselves and outsource other human resources work. This outsourcing process consists of hiring consultants or specialty firms to carry out activities in a particular area, such as payroll processors, recruitment firms, and compensation and benefits consultants. Described here are jobs at standalone firms providing human resources services.

Recruitment Firms

Recruitment firms, often called headhunters, are hired by companies to locate candidates for jobs. Recruitment firms are most often hired to fill managerial jobs, especially senior management, such as vice presidents. They are also used to locate professionals with particular scientific or technical skills. Some recruitment firms specialize in a particular industry such as information technology or health care. Others are generalists. When a company hires a recruitment firm to fill a position, the recruiter meets with the company's human resources personnel or management to obtain information on the position being filled and the requirements for applicants. The recruiter next locates potential candidates. The recruitment firm may have a pool of candidates consisting of people who have contacted the firm about work and provided their résumés. Recruiters may

A corporate recruiter conducts an online interview with an out-of-state job candidate. Modern computer technology has made new ways of locating and screening employees possible.

also place print and online ads. In addition, they often contact people who already have similar positions at other companies who may be interested in the job, especially if it involves a promotion or increase in pay.

Once a recruiter has assembled a pool of candidates, he or she will interview them at the recruitment company's office to see which candidates would best fit the job. The recruiter then arranges for interviews at the hiring firm. Once the hiring firm chooses a candidate, the recruitment firm receives a fee. Many recruitment firms have relationships with large companies they work with on a regular basis. Recruitment firms hire recruiters, support staff such as staffing assistants or coordinators, and sometimes account managers or representatives whose job it is to see that client companies' needs are met.

Benefits Management Firms

Firms today offer a number of different types of benefits to their employees. Among these are several types of insurance. Insurance can include health insurance, dental insurance, life insurance, and

INTERVIEWS WITH HUMAN RESOURCES PROFESSIONALS

The following excerpts from interviews with human resources professionals provide insight into the career of a human resources manager.

Lisa Rosendahl, a human resource director, supervises fourteen human resources employees for a large federal health care facility. In an interview on the Job Shadow Web site, she had this to say:

What does your work entail?

Technically, it entails staying current on the latest human resources practices, case law, policies, programs, and trends. Strategically, it's using that knowledge and my experiences to develop HR staff members and to work closely with facility leaders to address their pressing human resources issues, i.e., recruitment and hiring specialized staff, minimizing turnover, employee relations and labor relations. I am a certified mentor and am mentoring three employees and one HR professional in the community.

What's a typical workweek like?

On any given day, I could be developing our strategic workforce succession plan, meeting with an employee who has a question about her pay, reviewing a proposed disciplinary action or a grievance response, developing a position description for a new HR position, listening to a conference call about changes in our hiring process, gathering market data for a nurse's salary, or reviewing a request for reasonable accommodation.

What education, schooling, or skills are needed to do this?

Entry-level positions may require an associate's degree or its equivalent with zero to two years of experience in the field or in a related area, and HR generalist positions may require a bachelor's degree in a related area and zero to three years of experience in the field or in a related area. Although degrees are not often required, they are highly preferred in HR management positions along with five to seven years of progressively increasing responsibilities.

Carrie, a human resources manager for a high-end department store, shared her perspective on the job in an informational interview on the Career Planning Today Web site:

What do you do on a typical workday?

It varies every day. Every day is a busy workload. I do recruiting, hiring, training, firing, employee relations, benefits, payroll, United Way campaign, administrative, following through with employees, and their paperwork. We have to make sure we have all the right documents and all the right employees. I have to make sure we have qualified applicants. Sometimes I assist the department managers in their forty-five-day review with new employees and yearly reviews with each employee also.

What skills are required for your job?

Most of all patience, [being] prioritized and organized.

What activities do you enjoy doing the most?

Employee relations. I am a people person. I like to get to know employees. I like to go around and help managers and their salespeople work and teach them how to get promoted in a higher position.

What is the greatest challenge in your job?

The biggest challenge is being able to balance the workload. There is a lot of work to do, but you have to be able to prioritize what needs to be done and what else also needs to get done.

[Source: JobShadow.com. "Interview with a Human Resources Director." Retrieved February 12, 2013 (http://www.jobshadow.com/interview-with-a-human-resource-director).]

short- and long-term disability insurance, which provides pay to employees who are unable to work because of injury or health problems. These forms of insurance may be wholly paid by the company or partially paid by the company and employee. This

A benefits manager reviews charts and graphs to create projections of the company's needs for insurance in light of the number of anticipated employees given current economic conditions.

is especially true of health insurance. Therefore, many companies offer employees a choice of several different health insurance plans. Many firms hire benefit management firms to handle the process of investigating the insurance offerings of different companies and putting together a group of plans suitable for the company. Beyond this, many firms outsource the processing and tracking of insurance claims, especially health insurance claims. Some benefits management firms provide additional services to client companies, such as calculating and managing their contributions to plans such as workers' compensation insurance. Benefits management firms hire both staff with business, financial, or accounting degrees and support staff who perform functions such as entering financial data into computerized payroll systems. They also hire customer account representatives and managers, who are responsible for seeing that client companies' needs are met and resolving any problems that arise.

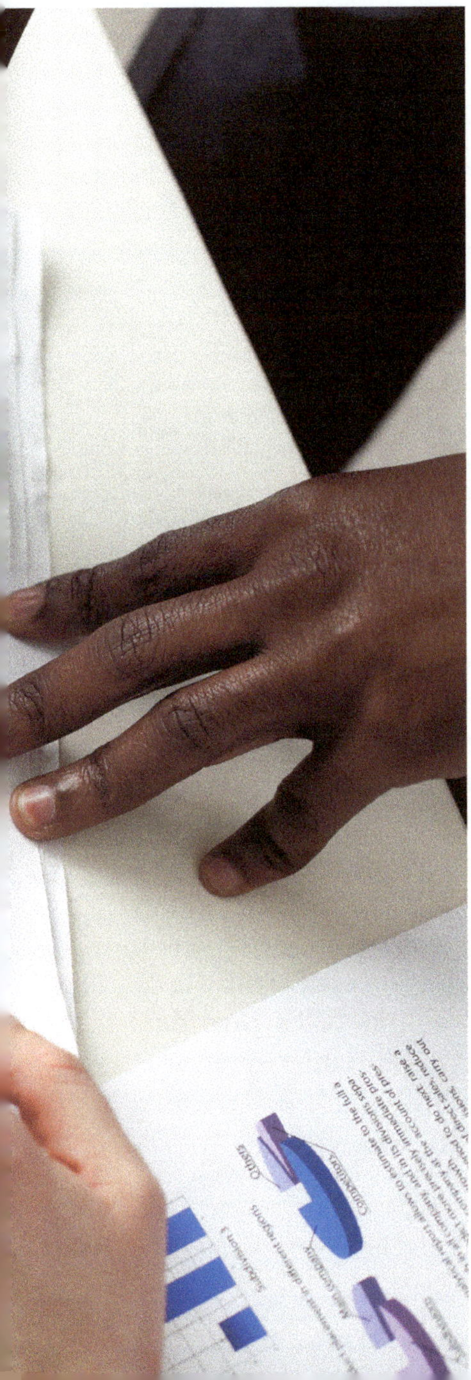

PAYROLL PROCESSING FIRMS

Payroll processing firms handle the payroll functions for client firms. They calculate the payroll

An employee at a payroll processing company runs paychecks for a client company's employees. The payroll processing company's staff members also provide direct-deposit services for many employees.

taxes and benefits plan deductions for employees and issue paychecks or directly deposit pay into employees' bank accounts. They also handle quarterly payroll tax processing for client companies. Payroll processing firms hire managers and consultants with degrees in accounting or finance. They also require support staff for entry-level or intermediate-level jobs. Like benefits management firms, payroll processing firms employ account representatives and managers who work with client companies to ensure that their needs are addressed. Some large human resources services companies, such as ADP, provide a variety of services to their clients. Such companies may offer payroll processing, benefits management, and even training services and may employ specialists in all these areas.

chapter 4

The Best Ways to Prepare for a Career in HR

A career in human resources requires a combination of business, communication, and people skills. There are courses students can take while in high school that will help them prepare for a job in human resources or further education in the field. In addition, one can engage in activities outside of school to gain experience and develop people-managing skills.

Laying the Groundwork

In a human resources job, a person will spend a great deal of time interacting with people—job candidates, employees, company management, consultants, and sometimes members of the public. Some of these encounters may occur under stressful circumstances. Therefore, the ability to communicate appropriately and clearly, both verbally and in writing, is very important.

Human resources professionals will find themselves creating and distributing written information on employee policies and events. In addition, they may be called on to write text for policy booklets or employee manuals. It is important to learn correct English grammar and syntax. One needs to understand the rules of English composition as well. These include how to structure one's writing so that it clearly conveys one's meaning. It is also useful to take a public speaking course. Such a course can help one feel more confident when speaking to groups and provide useful tips on structuring what is being said.

In the human resources field, professionals deal with people who come from a variety of different ethnic backgrounds. Many companies have employees from, and facilities in, different countries. It is essential for human resources professionals to understand the concerns and cultures of different people. Therefore, taking courses in history, especially world history, is indispensable. In addition, learning one or more languages other than English can be beneficial when applying for and performing a human resources job. With so many employees of different nationalities, language skills have become increasingly crucial in this field. Those in human resources may find themselves

Working on projects with people of different nationalities is common in today's global companies. Learning about other people's cultures can make such collaborations work smoothly.

working in areas of finance such as payroll and budgeting, as well as statistical analysis. Therefore, math courses such as algebra and statistics are helpful. In addition to preparing one for a job, having this academic background will make it easier for those who study human resources or business to succeed in college.

Human resources jobs require the use of computers. Everything from payroll to employee records must be entered into and retrieved from computer systems. Presentations are prepared on them, and various types of correspondence are written on them. Therefore, if the school offers a course in using computers, it's a good idea to take it, especially if it covers basic types of business software such as word processing and spreadsheets. For the same reason, it is a good idea to take a typing course if one is offered.

COMMUNICATION SKILLS

Few skills are more vital for a human resources professional than good communication skills. Developing good communication habits while in school can aid one later. Understanding employees depends on good listening techniques, which must be learned and require practice. There is a series of behaviors one can learn, called active listening techniques. These techniques can improve one's ability to hear and understand what others are saying.

These techniques start with paying attention to the person speaking—looking directly at the person, not at other things in the room. Listen to the speaker rather than thinking about how to respond. Nod or gesture to let the person know that what he or she is saying is being heard. Let the speaker finish speaking before responding. This shows respect and makes understanding easier. It's essential to confirm that one has understood the speaker correctly. Paraphrasing what the speaker has said allows the speaker to confirm that the listener has comprehended

CERTIFICATION

The HR Certification Institute offers various levels of certification for HR professionals, including those suitable for professional and senior-level HR staff, and global certification for those working with human resources in multiple countries. To be eligible for certification, one must have hands-on HR experience and pass an exam. The number of years of experience required varies according to educational level: the most years of experience are required for those with only a high school diploma and the least for those with a master's degree. For example, the basic Professional in Human Resources certification requires four years of experience for those with a high school diploma, two for those with a bachelor's degree, and one for those with a master's degree. The exams consist of 125 to 175 multiple-choice questions that cover areas such as business management and strategy, workforce planning and employment, human resources development, compensation and benefits, employee and labor relations, risk management, international hiring and compensation, and employee health and safety. Certification is valuable when looking for a job because it assures potential employers that one has the knowledge necessary to succeed in a position and that one is dedicated to the profession. In addition, because recertification is required periodically, having a current certification assures employers that an employee is up to date on the latest information regarding human resources practices and is broadening his or her knowledge. This continuing education is important because laws and regulations regarding human resources change frequently.

correctly. If unsure about what the speaker means, ask questions. Respond respectfully, even when disagreeing. Human resources professionals are often faced with this situation, so learning how to handle it now will be beneficial in the future.

Passing a certification exam can help an applicant when applying for a job. Certification organizations provide print and online resources to assist applicants in preparing for their exams.

It is useful to seek out situations where one can practice verbal communication. Any time spent in supporting a cause or engaging in debate will provide a chance to practice speaking skills. If speaking to a group, it can be helpful to ask for questions at the end of the talk, to clarify points that may have been misunderstood or that require further explanation. When speaking to individuals, it's useful to ask for their understanding of what was said to make sure they understood correctly. Learning good communication skills while in school will not

Students prepare materials for disaster relief. Seeking out opportunities to practice organizational and communication skills, such as organizing a charitable project, is a great way to learn human resources skills.

only help get a human resources job but will also help one be successful in that role.

GAINING EXPERIENCE

While still in high school, one can gain experience that will be useful in honing skills that apply to human resources. Being involved in almost any project working with other people to organize an event can provide such an opportunity. Organizing a school event, working on a political campaign, and helping produce a charity, sporting, or social action event can all help one gain experience before starting to look for a job. Such activities help to develop people management and organizational skills. They also provide experience that can be included on a résumé when applying for a job. The adults a person works with in such activities can provide references when applying for a job.

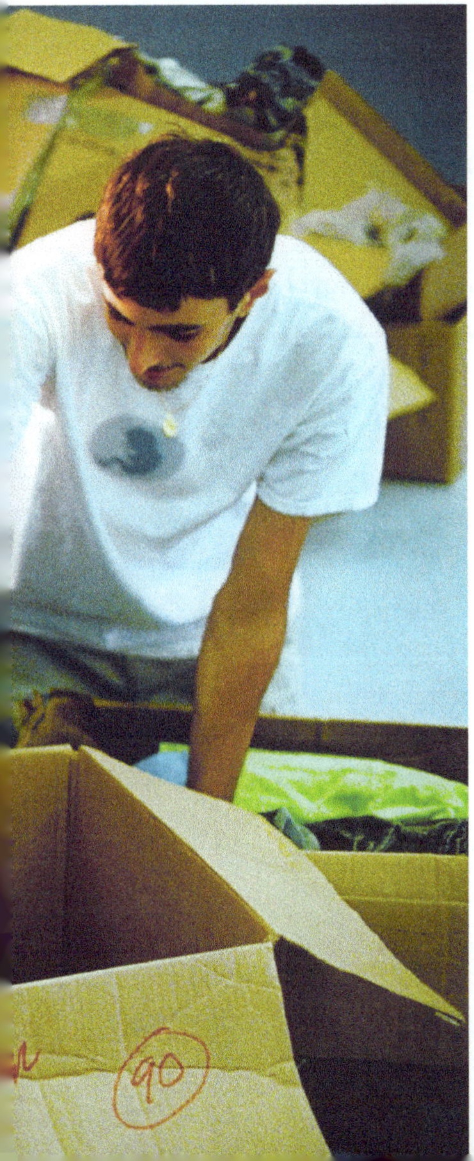

chapter 5

Education for an HR Career

There are various types of programs and training available for those interested in a human resources career. One can start a human resources career with various levels of educational training. Requirements for human resources positions range from a high school diploma and basic clerical skills to a master's degree. The more education in the field, the higher the level one can start at. Nevertheless, it is also possible to obtain additional education part-time while employed. Often companies offer tuition reimbursement programs in which they pay back employees for money spent taking courses or obtaining additional degrees related to their job.

College Programs

There are various educational paths that can be taken to prepare for a career in human resources. One can approach this career by obtaining an associate's degree and finding an entry-level job, with the option to continue education while working. Alternately, one can get a four-year degree and start as a human resources administrator. Whether pursuing a degree in human resources or business depends on one's long-term career goals. If a person wishes to concentrate on human resources as a lifelong career, then obtaining a bachelor's or even master's degree in human resources may provide the best option for advancement. If wishing to move into general management, then a bachelor's degree in business with a focus on human resources may be a good choice. Obtaining a general business degree is also a good option for those who wish to

Former football coach and U.S. congressman Tom Osborne teaches a business class at the University of Nebraska. Concentrating on a degree in business but with an emphasis on HR might be a good decision for you.

INTERNSHIPS

Internships are a great way to get a feel for what a job is like. In an internship, a student works with business professionals in an actual job environment. Most internships are unpaid, but they provide the opportunity to observe how professionals handle the tasks and issues that arise in the daily course of the job. Internships allow one to see if the field is appealing.

In addition to practical experience, internships allow students to form relationships with business professionals. These contacts may be able to assist the student later with finding a job or provide a recommendation. Many large companies offer internships. Information can often be found in the "Jobs" or "Careers" sections of their Web sites. For example, two major firms providing services to businesses, Xerox Corporation (http://www.xerox.com/jobs/student-internship-program/enus.html) and ADP (http://www.adp.com/careers/uscareers/work-at-adp/students-and-recent-graduates.aspx), offer internships for students. More information is available on their Web sites. Some college placement offices maintain information on internships. Also, Web sites such as InternMatch (http://www.internmatch.com/s/human-resources-internships) maintain information on internships.

become consultants in human resources. A business education provides knowledge of various aspects of running a business. If one wishes to pursue a career path that leads to senior management, then it is desirable to obtain a master's of business administration (MBA) degree. Some people go on to get an MBA directly after obtaining a bachelor's degree. Others obtain an MBA part-time while working, gaining experience while continuing their education.

An intern for an international company reviews a benefits form with her HR supervisor. HR internships can provide practical hands-on experience in real-life professional environments.

Associate's and bachelor's degree programs in human resources cover areas such as the recruitment and training of employees, workplace safety, compensation practices, benefits, labor laws, international human resources, and risk management. They also cover general business subjects such as business writing, management, organizational communications, and information systems. Another option is to pursue a bachelor's degree in business including courses on human resources. This degree includes a broader base of business courses, including courses in areas such as business law, management, and marketing, as well as courses on human resources.

Associate's degree programs are offered by technical schools and community colleges. Bachelor's and master's degree programs are offered by conventional colleges and universities. In addition, associate's degree and bachelor's degree programs are offered by online colleges. Obtaining a degree online is an especially attractive option for those who need to obtain a job directly out of high school but also wish to further their career. Obtaining a degree online or through a brick-and-mortar school while working improves one's chances of promotion or of getting a better job in another company. It's important to understand that obtaining a degree online requires a commitment to put in the same hours as one would in a conventional program, while working. If interested in pursuing a degree online, it's best to consult the U.S. Department of Education's database of accredited colleges (http://ope.ed.gov/accreditation). People can use this database to look up colleges by name to verify that an institution is accredited. Accreditation is necessary to obtain a valid degree or transfer credits to another school. In addition to degree programs, many colleges also offer certificate programs in human resources. These programs are designed to allow those who have majored in another area to gain skills in human resources.

SPECIFIC VS. GENERAL EDUCATION FOR HUMAN RESOURCES

Human resources professionals need to have an understanding of how people think and what motivates them. Moreover, today's human resources professionals work in an environment where employees come from diverse backgrounds. Human resources professionals will be more successful in dealing with employees, when issues arise, if they have an understanding of and sensitivity to cultural differences. For these reasons, taking courses in areas such as history, literature, sociology, and psychology can be beneficial. Learning a language other than English can also help one to communicate with employees from outside the United States.

Learning a language other than English can help one obtain a job in human resources, especially in areas where many employees are not native English speakers or in multinational companies.

PROFESSIONAL DEGREES

Some highly desirable jobs in human resources are available to those who have professional degrees in areas other than human resources or business. The laws and regulations covering the hiring and administration of the workforce have become increasingly complicated. Companies can face lawsuits by employees who were treated unfairly or incur fines for violating these laws. Therefore, there is a great need in the human resources field for individuals with a knowledge of labor and employment law. Private companies, and firms that provide consulting services to these companies, hire lawyers who specialize in law relating to labor and employment.

Finance professionals are also in demand in the human resources field. Firms providing compensation and benefits services to companies employ those with a degree in finance, economics, or accounting as managers and consultants to their client companies. Private companies also employ individuals with these degrees to manage areas such as benefits administration and compensation.

chapter 6

Paths for Pursuing an HR Career

There are a number of strategies for getting a job in the human resources field and maximizing the chances of success once employed, whether one decides to pursue a job directly after high school or go on to college. This material covers approaches for finding a job and ways to maximize one's chances of being successful in the field.

Getting Your First Job

Most people think of checking want ads when they are considering looking for a job. Today, most newspapers offer access to want ads in both their print and online versions. It may be worthwhile to send a résumé in response to want ads while also pursuing other options for locating a job. However, this is often the least effective way to land a job. Companies often receive enormous numbers of résumés in response to their ads, especially in a difficult economy. From this pile of résumés, they select only a few applicants to interview, often choosing those with the most experience, who are already performing a job like the one they are trying to fill.

More important for the job seeker, only a small portion of available jobs are listed in ads. Many jobs are filled before they are advertised. Companies find candidates through word of mouth, recommendations from employees, or unsolicited résumés sent to the company. In addition to answering ads, there are a number of other ways to find a job.

COLLEGE PLACEMENT AND JOB FAIRS

Many colleges and technical schools, including online ones, have a placement office. This office helps students locate jobs. The placement office may also have workshops on other aspects of job hunting, such as résumé and interview preparation. It's also common for colleges to host job fairs to which a variety of companies send representatives to discuss job openings with graduating students. Because most companies require human resources personnel, it is worth talking with

A professional-looking résumé can help get an interview. At the interview, personal presentation is important in convincing the interviewer that one is a serious professional.

these company representatives about potential openings in their human resources departments, even if these types of jobs aren't specifically being advertised. In some cases, communities hold job fairs as well, and these job fairs are also worth attending.

DISTRIBUTING RÉSUMÉS

Because the majority of companies hire human resources staff, it is possible to identify specific types of companies

Job fairs provide an opportunity to distribute résumés to companies of interest and obtain information about companies that one might not have been aware of.

and industries, and then apply for a job. One can find companies that might be interesting to work for from a variety of sources. If one is interested in working in a particular industry, such as health care, energy, sports, and the like, it is often possible to obtain a directory of companies in that industry from an industry association. It is also possible to obtain a list of companies in a given industry by doing an online search. Another approach is to use a general business directory to locate companies that might be of interest. For example, many libraries have a list of the Dow Jones or Standard & Poor's directories of companies. These books provide the address, industry, size, and other information about a large number of companies. After identifying companies of interest, one can send a résumé to the director of human resources, with a cover letter expressing interest in working at that company. In some cases there may be an opening. Even if there is not, it is common for managers to keep a file of résumés that have been received and refer to them when an opening arises. Persistence is the key to obtaining job interviews. One may need to send out a large number of résumés and keep sending more out each week before getting a job.

ONLINE JOB SEARCHES

Many companies post job openings online. Many use job-hunting sites such as Monster.com, Indeed.com, and CareerBuilder.com. Such listings are less expensive for companies and reach a very large audience of tech-savvy young professionals. To see what jobs are available in human resources in an area, simply type "human resources" and the city or state in the search box on these sites. These sites can be searched for jobs locally, statewide, or nationally, or by a specific job title, such as human resources assistant, coordinator, or manager; benefits manager; or recruiter. Alternately, one can simply choose to see all human resources jobs.

Social networking can also be used to find potential jobs. LinkedIn is a social networking site used primarily for business contact purposes. It has become a valuable source of job postings. In addition to postings on job-hunting sites, many companies post job openings on their own company Web sites. Agencies of the U.S. government post job listings online as well, so check out their Web sites. To view job openings, click on the "Jobs," "Careers," or similar link on the company's or agency's Web site.

Larger companies often use recruitment agencies to fill jobs, especially for managerial positions. A search can be done for recruitment agencies in a given city, either online or in the phone book. One can then send a résumé to the recruitment company.

NETWORKING

One of the best ways to find a job is through networking—talking with people who might know of job openings. Networking can take several forms. One way of networking is to ask family and friends if they know of any job openings in HR at the companies they work for or ask for the name of the HR manager at their company. Another way of networking is to join a business organization in one's area, such as the chamber of commerce, local business council, or rotary club, or a human resources professional organization such as the National Human Resources Association (www.humanresources.org). Going to the meetings sponsored by these organizations gives one the chance to meet professionals in the industry and discuss possible job openings. In addition, many of these companies provide information on job openings and other career assistance to their members. It can be useful to join such organizations while in school and participate in their activities. When attending meetings, it's useful to get the names, e-mail addresses, and business cards of people one meets, so they can be contacted later when

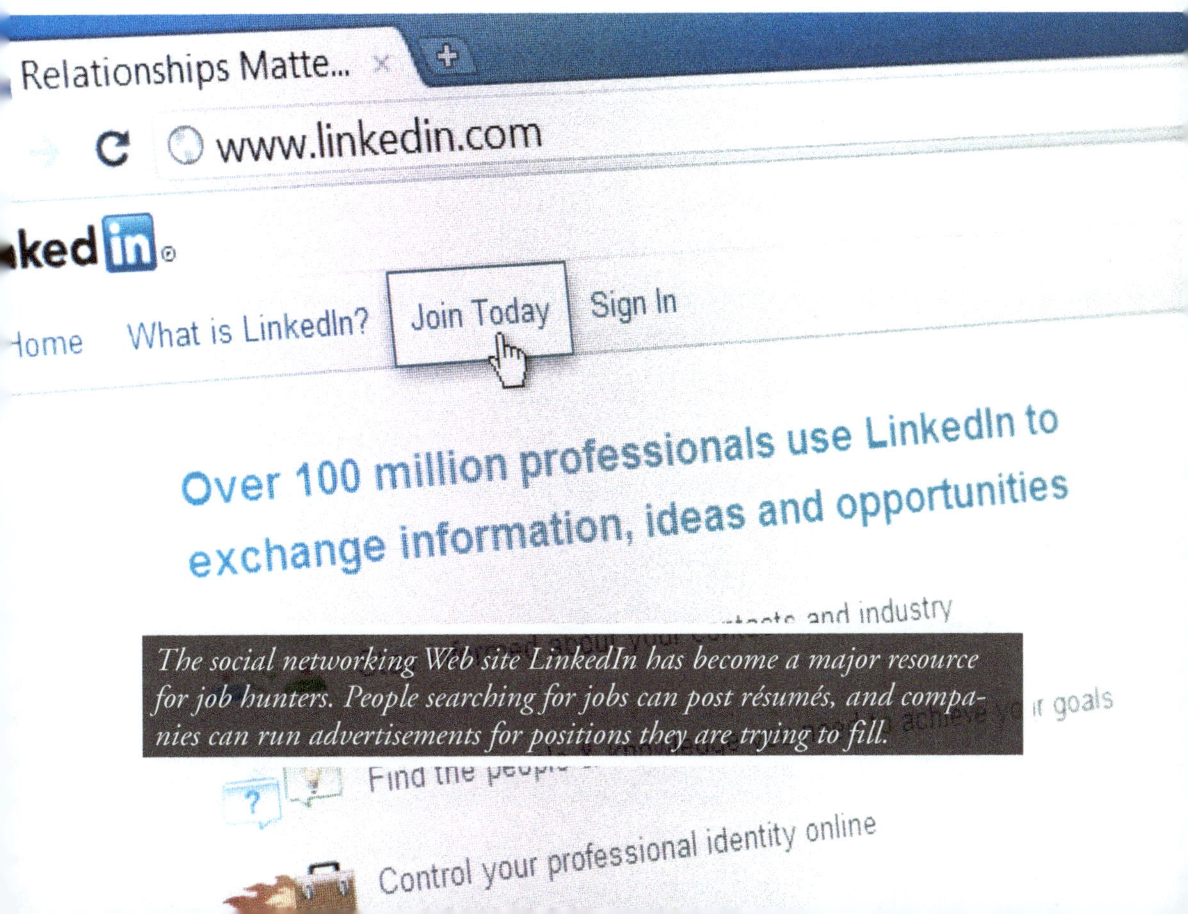

The social networking Web site LinkedIn has become a major resource for job hunters. People searching for jobs can post résumés, and companies can run advertisements for positions they are trying to fill.

Sarah Mendez
197 South Street
Worcester, Massachusetts 01601
Home: (508) 555-1212 Cell: (508) 555-2000
smendez@isp.net

Objective: A position as a human resources manager where I can use my experience and expertise to implement and manage human resources programs to allow the company to make effective use of its employees.

Professional Experience

International Technology Corporation, Bellevue, MA 2011–Present
Personnel Administrator

Worked with senior management to create HR policies and procedures to ensure compliance with state and federal laws. Wrote employee manual to ensure employees and managers had knowledge of appropriate code of conduct, disciplinary procedures, and information on benefits.
Recruited employees and developed orientation, training, and incentive programs to maximize employee effectiveness.
Created benefits database; administer benefits and leave-of-absence programs.
Administered benefits enrollment and programs.
Tracked HR expenditures to ensure compliance with HR budget. Negotiated salary offers, including relocation packages for both exempt and nonexempt employees.
Brought workers' compensation program into full compliance. Instituted preferred providers list and trained managers and associates on procedures to follow in case of injury.
Streamlined the company's performance review program, creating a flexible and well-received tool that was later adopted company-wide.
Created standardized job descriptions across the company to provide an accurate picture of the duties and skills required for each position.
Trained managers in interviewing techniques and best practices, conducting workshops and one-on-one sessions that contributed to sound hiring decisions.
Interfaced with senior personnel from outside firm that provides payroll-processing services to ensure timely and accurate performance.

Consolidated Widget Corporation, Worcester, MA 2008–2010
Human Resources Representative

Placed print and online advertisements to recruit employees. Worked with recruitment agency to locate candidates for senior management and high-level technical positions.
Developed training and orientation materials.
Administered employee benefits database and managed human resources records.
Resolved conflicts between employees and insurance carriers and coordinated health fairs to promote employee wellness.
Codeveloped company's first-ever standardized disciplinary procedures and tracking system that insulated company from legal risk and ensured consistent and fair discipline processes.
Devised creative and cost-effective incentive and morale-boosting programs (including special events and a tiered awards structure) that increased employee satisfaction and productivity.
Reworked new-hire orientation program to include HR information and information on company resources.

Education

Worcester High School, 2008
Bachelor's degree, University of Massachusetts, 2012, Human Resources Management
Certified professional in human resources (PHR)

Additional Skills

Human resources information system applications: UltiPro, PeopleSoft Enterprise Human Resources, ADP
Microsoft Office: Word, Excel, PowerPoint, Access, Outlook
Fluent in Spanish

References available on request

looking for a job. Even if they do not have a job opening, they may know of another company that does.

PREPARING A RÉSUMÉ

The major tool for getting a job is the résumé. A résumé is one- or two-page document that lists one's qualifications for a job, including education, work experience, and special skills. The purpose of a résumé is to convince a potential employer to arrange a job interview. The following are some ways to maximize the effect of a résumé:

- Use a simple, easy-to-read format. Such a format allows potential employers to find one's work and educational experience easily. There are many trendy formats for résumés, but when you are looking for your first or second job, it's best to avoid these. Employers, especially those in human resources, are often wise to attempts to disguise an applicant's lack of experience. Instead, applicants should focus their attention on the skills, education, and experience they have that are relevant.
- Research the industry, the company, and the job being applied for. The Internet has made it easy to find out everything one needs to know about a company and industry. Start by checking the company's own Web site, which will provide a wealth of information. A general search on the company's name can bring up articles about the company that provide additional information on its activities.

At left is an example of a résumé for a human resources manager position. Successful résumés clearly and concisely detail the applicant's experience, skills, and qualities that can benefit a company.

- Emphasize skills and experience that apply specifically to that industry, company, and job. Explain why your experience or knowledge would help you succeed in the position. For instance, if you fluently speak a language other than English, mention this if you are applying to work in a multinational company or in a location in the United States where many people speak that language.
- Don't just list the jobs or volunteer positions you have held. Instead, explain what you accomplished in those positions. For instance, rather than saying "volunteered with XYZ charity," say "organized twenty-five volunteers for road race to raise money for XYZ charity and made sure that runners had adequate supplies." Explaining how one has made a program more effective or efficient shows employers that an applicant understands the concerns of a company. Demonstrating the ability to work with people shows that an applicant has human resources skills.
- Those who are applying for a job directly after high school must convince potential employers that they can handle the job, despite not having much previous work experience. To show they have adequate education to handle the job, applicants should list relevant courses that they have taken in high school. These will vary according to the industry in which the company operates. For example, when applying to a health care company, such courses might include biology, chemistry, and physics. Applicants should note if they have taken computer courses or have a knowledge of common office software such as word processing,

spreadsheet, and presentation programs. Applicants should also include any vocational courses or programs such as a business technology that provide relevant skills and any foreign languages they speak fluently.

- One shouldn't include irrelevant personal information. The exception is hobbies or experiences that are related to the company's industry or products. For example, if the company makes skis and an applicant is an expert skier, or if the company is in the alternative energy field and an applicant has been active in promoting ecological concerns by working with one of the nonprofits in the field, he or she should mention this. If an applicant has donated time to charitable organizations, he or she should mention that. Companies today wish to be seen as good corporate citizens, and volunteering demonstrates that an applicant is the kind of person who is willing to assist others, not just him- or herself. Also, if one has won an award, this is worth mentioning. Even if it was in an area that isn't related to what the company does, this type of achievement shows that the person is a hard worker and can follow through.
- Above all, it is important to make sure that the résumé is neat and professional looking. Applicants should proofread their work or have someone else read it. Do not just rely on spelling/grammar-checking software. It will miss errors such as the use of "hole" for "whole" because "hole" is a real word. Employers assume that people who send in résumés that are sloppy and contain mistakes will produce work with the same flaws.

THE INTERVIEW

If an applicant is asked to come in for an interview, that is his or her opportunity to convince a prospective employer that he or she is the right person for the job. The first consideration when going to an interview is appearance. This meeting is the first impression the applicant will make on the interviewer. Applicants should dress in business-appropriate clothing and be well groomed.

Staff members conduct a group interview with a job candidate. It is common for candidates to be interviewed by various department members to ensure a good fit with existing employees.

During the interview the applicant should speak calmly and respectfully. If asked about skills or experience they don't have, applicants should explain why their education or previous experience equips them to learn those skills. Interviewers sometimes ask questions designed to see how applicants solve problems or behave under stress. What the interviewer is really interested in is not a solution to the problem posed, but how the applicant responds to such problems. The applicant should demonstrate that he or she

TIPS FOR GETTING A FIRST JOB

The following tips are adapted from "Tips for Getting Your First Job" by the Minnesota Department of Employment and Economic Development:

1. **List places to apply:** Gather possibilities from sources such as print and online ads, job banks, career centers, job Web sites, employment agencies, job fairs, newspapers, networking contacts, and high school guidance or college career centers.
2. **Gather your information:** Be prepared to provide information on when you are available and how you can be reached, your résumé, and a list of references.
3. **Make a good first impression**: Make sure your appearance is appropriate. Personal grooming and the way you dress can matter more than a smart interview answer. Don't slump or chew gum. Turn off your cell phone. Show interest in the job and company and a willingness to learn.
4. **Use an appropriate, simple e-mail address:** Employers don't want to contact someone at SuperHotGuy@hottie.com for an interview. This type of e-mail address is considered unprofessional.
5. **Be persistent:** As a first-time job seeker, prepare yourself to hear "no." Don't be discouraged by rejection. Nobody receives a job offer for every job application that he or she submits. Remember to ask to be contacted if another opening occurs, leave a copy of your résumé, and thank the employer for his or her time.
6. **Get experience:** A little experience can go a long way. Getting some types of work experience as early as possible

makes you a stronger job candidate. Experience mowing lawns or babysitting shows that you know how to keep commitments, be on time, and do high-quality work.

7. **Think of your future goals:** Start thinking about a career that would allow you to achieve the lifestyle you want while doing what you're really good at. Try to work part-time or volunteer now in areas that relate to a career you are interested in.

can analyze the problem and consider what it might be possible to do.

There are many different questions an interviewer could ask. The following are examples of some common ones:

- Why are you qualified for this job, or what qualities do you have that would make you successful in this job? Before going to the interview, applicants should study the company and job listing. They should then prepare a mental list of experience, education, and personal qualities that would make them successful in the position. When questioned, they can go through their mental list and explain why they can meet each qualification.
- Are you a self-starter, or can you work without supervision? Applicants should give examples of situations

in which they were given responsibilities at work, or when volunteering, that demonstrate their ability to take the initiative or work without supervision.

- What are your strengths? This is an opportunity to discuss your strong points in terms of education, experience, or personal traits.
- What is your greatest weakness? This question is designed to see how you respond to a difficult situation, more than to elicit an actual weakness. An appropriate answer is: "I'm impatient—I can't stand sitting around without something to do." This type of answer has the advantage of being believable while turning a weakness into a benefit.

When answering interview questions, think about why the interviewer is asking the question, and respond to what he or she really wants to know. For example, if applicants are asked a question that suggests the interviewer may think that they are too young to do the job, an appropriate response is, "I know I am recently out of school, but I have the most recent knowledge about the field, and I am mature, organized, and disciplined."

BEING PROFESSIONAL

In human resources, one is always dealing with other people, including members of the public. Therefore, personal presentation is very important. How applicants dress can influence an interviewer who is deciding whether or not they know how to conduct themselves in a business environment where they are representing the company. Therefore, it is important that an applicant's dress, attitude, and behavior be

Dressing professionally is important for human resources job candidates because HR staff members work with people, who are likely to judge whether or not they are professional based on personal presentation.

professional. When attending an interview, men should wear slacks, a dress shirt and tie, and a jacket. For higher-level positions, wearing a suit may be appropriate. Women should wear a business-appropriate dress, skirt and blouse, or suit. One should avoid overly tight-fitting or revealing clothes. Hair should be neatly cut, and one should not wear loud makeup or jewelry, or piercings. One's shoes should be clean and polished.

Human resources professionals should always treat people they meet with respect. On the job they must deal tactfully with people of different genders, races, and ethnicities. So demonstrating this at the interview and when meeting members of the staff will reassure potential employers that one understands how to behave.

PARTICIPATING IN PROFESSIONAL ORGANIZATIONS

There are several professional organizations devoted to furthering the interests of professionals in human resources. Among them are: the National Human Resources Association (NHRA), Professionals in Human Resources Association (PIHRA), the International Association of Administrative Professionals (IAAP), and the Society for Human Resource Management (SHRM). These organizations provide a variety of resources for their members to help them develop and improve their skills. Often they also offer career-related resources. In addition, they may produce publications that keep members up to date on the latest knowledge and techniques. Some hold conferences at which members can share information. Some have special memberships, information on internships, or scholarships for students. Joining a professional organization can help one improve one's skills and learn new ones. By attending conferences and conventions, one can learn from experts in the field. Participation also provides the opportunity to network with others in the field and get help in dealing with issues when they arise. Participating in the organization also gives a person the chance to contribute to the field, by sharing knowledge gained on the job, writing articles for journals published by the organization, presenting papers at conferences, and working to create standards for the field.

glossary

Americans with Disabilities Act A law passed in 1990 that requires employers to make reasonable accommodation to all people with disabilities.

asset Something of value, such as a stock or bond.

bond A form of debt in which a person gives money to a company and the company pays interest on that money to the person until it pays the original amount back.

chronic Occurring continuously over a long period of time.

compensation The combination of cash and other items of value, such as stock, given to employees in return for their work.

confidentiality agreement A document signed by employees in which they agree to keep company information secret.

diverse Different from each other; various.

equal employment opportunity laws Laws, such as Title VII of the Civil Rights Act of 1964, that prohibit discrimination against women and minorities and require equal treatment in the workplace.

financial services company A company that manages investments.

401(k) retirement plan A plan in which employees can invest a portion of their pay through a company-provided plan, so that they will have money for retirement. Usually the company matches a percentage of the employees' contribution.

insurance An arrangement by which a company or the state untertakes to provide a guarantee of compensation for specified loss, damage, illness, or death in return for payment of a specified premium.

job bank A collection of job openings maintained by an organization such as a state department of employment.

letter of agreement A letter sent to a person being offered a job that spells out the pay and other aspects of the job being offered.

motivate The process of making people feel that they want to perform an activity.

noncompete agreement A document signed by an employee in which he or she agrees not to engage in an activity that directly competes with the company if he or she leaves.

orientation The process of familiarizing an employee with the people, facilities, and procedures of a company.

outsource To hire a person or company to perform activities instead of using employees to perform them.

paraphrase To rephrase what a person has said or written.

pension fund An investment fund maintained by a company to provide money to retired employees.

performance review A periodic evaluation of how well an employee has carried out his or her responsibilities.

policy handbook A binder or booklet that contains descriptions of the policies that employees are expected to follow.

predecessor A person or company that previously held the same position as the present entity.

professional development Providing employees with additional training and support to allow them to advance in their careers.

recruitment The process of attracting potential employees.

regulatory agency A government organization that issues rules governing the behavior of companies and monitors compliance with the rules.

screen To compare the qualifications of applicants against a list of requirements to choose the most appropriate candidates.
stabilize Keep from constantly changing.
stock An investment representing a small share of a company. If the company's value increases, so does the stock.
strategic planning The process by which company management identifies the goals of a company and the means to achieve them.
syntax The rules that govern proper usage of a language.
termination The act of firing an employee.
trait A physical or personality-related characteristic.
unsolicited Not requested.

for more information

American Management Association
1601 Broadway #7
New York, NY 10036
(212) 586-8100
Web site: http://www.amanet.org
This organization provides certificate programs and online seminars for business professionals, including those in human resources. It also offers an array of books and other resources.

American Society for Training and Development (ASTD)
1640 King Street, Box 1443
Alexandria, VA 22313-1443
(800) 628-2783 or (703) 683-8100
Web site: http://www.astd.org
The ASTD provides publications and educational resources on employee training and development, as well as certification in this area.

Canadian Council of Human Resource Associations
130 Slater Street, Suite 1025
Ottawa, ON K1P 6E2
Canada
(613) 567-2477 or (866) 560-1288
Web site: http://www.cchra.ca
This is a collection of human resources associations from across Canada, which represent more than forty-one thousand professionals. It holds events that allow human resources professionals to network with each other and works to further the profession.

Human Resources Certification Institute
1800 Duke Street
Alexandria, VA 22314
(866) 898-4724
Web site: http://www.hrci.org
This organization provides certification of human resources professionals and job postings on its Web site.

International Association of Administrative Professionals (IAAP)
10502 North Ambassador Drive, Suite 100
Kansas City, MO 64153
(816) 891-6600
Web site: http://www.iaap-hq.org
Founded in 1942, the International Association of Administrative Professionals provides administrative professionals with opportunities for growth, networking, education, and development, including education, certification, publications, and job postings on its Web site.

National Human Resources Association (NHRA)
P.O. Box 5455
Manchester, NH 03108-5455
(866) 523-4417
Web site: http://www.humanresources.org
Established in 1951, the NHRA supports the professional development of human resource professionals. It provides job listings on its Web site.

Professionals In Human Resources Association (PIHRA)
360 North Sepulveda Boulevard, Suite 2020
El Segundo, CA 90245
(310) 416-1210
Web site: http://www.pihra.org

The PIHRA, founded in 1944, provides human resources professionals with the opportunity to collaborate and enhance the profession. It holds conferences, provides certification exams, and lists news and job listings on its Web site.

Society for Human Resource Management (SHRM)
1800 Duke Street
Alexandria, VA 22314
(800) 283-7476
Web site: http://www.shrm.org
SHRM is dedicated to serving the needs of human resources management professionals through certification, conferences, research, publications, and other resources.

U.S. Bureau of Labor Statistics (BLS)
Postal Square Building
2 Massachusetts Avenue NE
Washington, DC 20212
(202) 691-5200
Web site: http://www.bls.gov
An agency within the U.S. Department of Labor, the BLS is responsible for calculating labor market activity, working conditions, and price changes in the U.S. economy. It provides essential information about the U.S. workforce and careers.

U.S. Department of Labor (DOL)
Frances Perkins Building
200 Constitution Avenue NW
Washington, DC 20210
Web site: http://www.dol.gov
This department of the U.S. government provides information on all aspects of labor in the United States.

Workplace.ca
1081 Ambleside Drive, Suite 2210
Ottawa, ON K2B 8C8
Canada
(613) 721-5957
Web site: http://www.workplace.ca
This division of the Institute of Professional Management (IPM) provides training, publications, and other resources for human resources professionals in Canada.

WEB SITES

Due to the changing nature of Internet links, Rosen Publishing has developed an online list of Web sites related to the subject of this book. This site is updated regularly. Please use this link to access the list:

http://www.rosenlinks.com/EC/Human

for further reading

Armstrong, Sharon, and Barbara Mitchell. *The Essential HR Handbook*. Franklin Lakes, NJ: The Career Press, 2008.

Bolles, Richard N. *What Color Is Your Parachute? A Practical Manual for Job-Hunters and Career Changers*. 2013 ed. New York, NY: Ten Speed Press/Random House, 2013.

Collins, Alan. *Unwritten HR Rules: 21 Secrets for Attaining Awesome Career Success in Human Resources*. Chicago, IL: Success in HR Publishing, 2011.

Crompton, Diane, and Ellen Sautter. *Finding a Job Through Social Networking*. Indianapolis, IN: JIST Publishing, 2010.

DelCampo, Robert G. *Human Resource Management DeMYSTiFieD*. New York, NY: McGraw-Hill, 2010.

DeLuca, Matthew, and Nannette DeLuca. *Best Answers to the 201 Most Frequently Asked Interview Questions*. New York, NY: McGraw-Hill, 2010.

Fry, Ron. *101 Great Answers to the Toughest Interview Questions*. Boston, MA: Course Technology, 2009.

Kennedy, Joyce Lain. *Cover Letters for Dummies*. Hoboken, NJ: Wiley, 2009.

Kennedy, Joyce Lain. *Job Interviews for Dummies*. Hoboken, NJ: Wiley, 2011.

Labovich, Laura. *100 Conversations for Career Success: Learn to Network, Cold Call, and Tweet Your Way to Your Dream Job*. New York, NY: LearningExpress, 2012.

McKinney, Anne. *Real-Resumes for Human Resources & Personnel Jobs*. Fayetteville, NC: PREP Publishing, 2012.

Mesmer, Max. *Human Resources Kit for Dummies*. Hoboken, NJ: Wiley, 2012.

Pollak, Lindsey. *Getting from College to Career: Your Essential Guide to Succeeding in the Real World*. New York, NY: HarperCollins, 2012.

Rivers, Ford R. *Get the Job You Want, Even When No One's Hiring*. Hoboken, NJ: Wiley, 2009.

Waldman, Joshua. *Job Searching with Social Media for Dummies*. Hoboken, NJ: Wiley, 2011.

bibliography

Armstrong, Sharon, and Barbara Mitchell. *The Essential HR Handbook*. Pompton Plains, NJ: Career Press, 2008.

CareerBuilder.com. "Human Resources." Retrieved February 10, 2013 (http://human-resources.careerbuilder.com).

Career Planning Today. "Human Resource Manager: Informational Interview Report." December 30, 2009. Retrieved February 22, 2013 (http://careerplanningtoday.com/2009/12/30/human-resource-manager-informational-interview-report).

Free Management Library. "All About Human Resources and Talent Management." Retrieved February 13, 2013 (http://managementhelp.org/humanresources/index.htm).

Human Resources Certification Institute. *Certification Handbook*. Retrieved February 19, 2013 (http://www.hrci.org/uploadedfiles/Content/Resource_Library/Certification_Handbooks_and_Other_Publications/2010%20Certification%20Handbook.pdf).

JobShadow.com. "Interview with a Human Resources Director." Retrieved February 12, 2013 (http://www.jobshadow.com/interview-with-a-human-resource-director).

Management Study Guide. "Human Resource Management." Retrieved February 13, 2013 (http://www.managementstudyguide.com/human-resource-management.htm).

Mayhew, Ruth. "Primary Responsibilities of a Human Resource Manger." *Houston Chronicle*. Retrieved February 8, 2013 (http://smallbusiness.chron.com/primary-responsibilities-human-resource-manager-10957.html).

McGraw-Hill Higher Education. "Bachelor in Human Resources." Retrieved February 20, 2013 (http://www

.mhhe.com/education/program/business/human-resources/bachelor.html).

Minnesota Department of Employment and Economic Development. "Tips for Getting Your First Job." Retrieved February 22, 2013 (http://www.iseek.org/jobs/firstjob.html).

Noe, Raymond, John Hollenbeck, Gary Gerhart, and Patrick Wright. *Human Resource Management*. New York, NY: McGraw-Hill, 2009.

Princeton Review. "A Day in the Life of a Human Resource Manager." Retrieved February 14, 2013 (http://www.princetonreview.com/careers.aspx?cid=78).

Rasmussen College. "Top Professional Organizations for Business Students." Retrieved February 20, 2013 (http://www.rasmussen.edu/degrees/business/blog/top-professional-associations-for-business-students).

Society for Human Resource Management. "Careers in Human Resource Management." Retrieved February 14, 2013 (http://www.shrm.org/Communities/StudentPrograms/Pages/careersinHRM.aspx).

U.S. Department of Labor Bureau of Labor Statistics. *Occupational Outlook Handbook*, 2012–2013. Retrieved February 12, 2013 (http://www.bls.gov/ooh).

index

S

T

U

V

W

X

ABOUT THE AUTHOR

Jeri Freedman has a B.A. degree from Harvard University. She has more than fifteen years of experience in sales and marketing for high-tech companies. She is the author of numerous young adult nonfiction books, including *Women in the Workplace: Wages, Respect, and Equal Rights* and *Being a Leader: Organizing and Inspiring a Group*.

PHOTO CREDITS

Cover (figure) Yuri Arcurs/Shutterstock.com; cover (background), p. 1 © iStockphoto.com/Daniel Mirer; p. 4 Robert Churchill/the Agency Collection/Getty Images; p. 8 Library of Congress Prints and Photographs Division; p. 10 © Jeff Greenberg/The Image Works; p. 12 The Washington Post/ Getty Images; pp. 14, 30–31 Pressmaster/Shutterstock.com; p. 16 Lisa S./Shuttterstock.com; p. 18 EdBookStock/ Shutterstock.com; p. 20 Hyoung Chang/The Denver Post/ Getty Images; pp. 22–23, 58–59 Franz Pfluegl/Shutterstock.com; p. 24 wavebreakmedia/Shutterstock.com; pp. 26–27 mast3r/Shutterstock.com; pp. 32, 40–41 © AP Images; p. 34 Chris Clinton/Digital Vision/Thinkstock; p. 37 Mihai Blanaru/Shutterstock.com; pp. 38–39 Jeff Greenberg/ Photolibrary/Getty Images; p. 43 F1online/Thinkstock; p. 45 Image Source/Getty Images; pp. 48–49 Ariel Skelley/Blend Images/Getty Images; pp. 50–51 Justin Sullivan/Getty Images; p. 53 SimplyCreativePhotography/Shutterstock.com; p. 63 Comstock/Thinkstock; back cover (background) © iStockphoto.com/blackred.

Designer: Matt Cauli; Editor: Kathy Kuhtz Campbell;
Photo Researcher: Marty Levick